10/04

GIANT PLANT-EATING DINOSAURS

BY "DINO" DON LESSEM

ILLUSTRATIONS BY JOHN BINDON

LERNER PUBLICATIONS COMPANY / MINNEAPOLIS

To Jack McIntosh, a giant in the study of giant dinosaurs

Text copyright © 2005 by Dino Don, Inc.
Illustrations copyright © 2005 by John Bindon
Photographs courtesy of: Professor Rodolfo Coria, Museo Carmen Funes, Plaza Huincul, Argentina, p. 21;
© Dino Don, Inc., pp. 29–31.

This book is available in two editions:
Library binding by Lerner Publications Company,
    a division of Lerner Publishing Group
Soft cover by First Avenue Editions,
    an imprint of Lerner Publishing Group
241 First Avenue North
Minneapolis, MN 55401 U.S.A.

Website address: www.lernerbooks.com

Library of Congress Cataloging-in-Publication-Data

Lessem, Don.
  Giant plant-eating dinosaurs / by Don Lessem ; illustrations by John Bindon.
      p.   cm. — (Meet the dinosaurs)
  Includes index.
  ISBN: 0-8225-1371-4 (lib. bdg. : alk. paper)
  ISBN: 0-8225-2573-9 (pbk. : alk. paper)
    1. Dinosaurs—Juvenile literature. 2. Herbivores, Fossil—Juvenile literature. I. Bindon, John. II. Title.
  QE861.5.L477 2005
  567.9—dc22   2004004453

Manufactured in the United States of America
1 2 3 4 5 6 – DP – 10 09 08 07 06 05

TABLE OF CONTENTS

MEET THE GIANT PLANT EATERS

WELCOME, DINOSAUR FANS!

I'm "Dino" Don. I LOVE dinosaurs. The giant plant eaters are among my favorites. I helped dig up the bones of the biggest one of all! Come meet some of these amazing giants.

APATOSAURUS (uh-PAT-uh-SAWR-uhs)
Length: 85 feet
Home: western North America
Time: 145 million years ago

ARGENTINOSAURUS (AHR-jehn-TEE-nuh-SAWR-uhs)
Length: 120 feet
Home: Argentina, South America
Time: 100 million years ago

BRACHIOSAURUS (BRAK-ee-uh-SAWR-uhs)
Length: 84 feet
Home: western North America
Time: 145 million years ago

DIPLODOCUS (DIHP-luh-DOH-kuhs)
Length: 100 feet
Home: western North America
Time: 145 million years ago

SALTASAURUS (SAHL-tuh-SAWR-uhs)
Length: 40 feet
Home: South America
Time: 83 million years ago

SEISMOSAURUS (SYZ-muh-SAWR-uhs)
Length: 125 feet
Home: southwestern North America
Time: 145 million years ago

SHUNOSAURUS (SHOO-nuh-SAWR-uhs)
Length: 46 feet
Home: eastern Asia
Time: 175 million years ago

GIANTS OF THE PAST

Let's travel back in time to the forests of
South America, 100 million years ago.
You're standing in the shadow of a
creature the size of an apartment building.
It is alive—and it is under attack!

Enormous plant-eating dinosaurs such as
Argentinosaurus were the biggest animals
ever to walk the earth. Yet they were not
safe from attack. *Argentinosaurus* must
fight off *Giganotosaurus,* the king of the
meat eaters, to survive.

THE TIME OF THE GIANT PLANT EATERS

Shunosaurus

Seismosaurus

175 million
years ago

145 million
years ago

Dinosaurs such as *Argentinosaurus* lived on land long before humans did. The first dinosaurs appeared nearly 230 million years ago. Some ate meat. Others were **herbivores,** animals that eat plants. Some plant eaters grew to huge sizes.

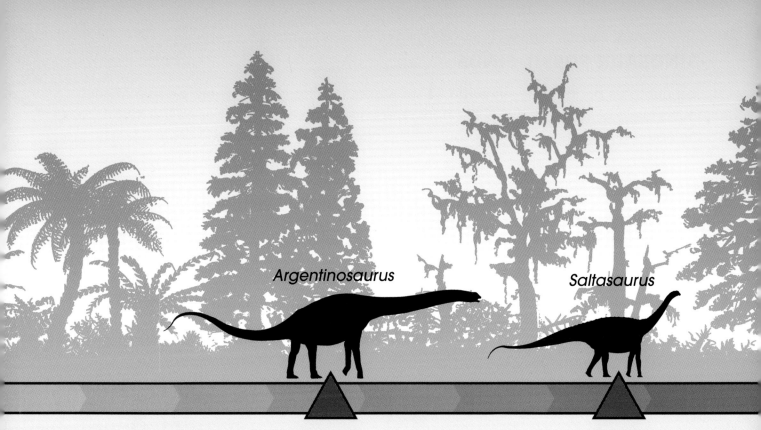

Argentinosaurus

Saltasaurus

100 million
years ago

83 million
years ago

The giant plant eaters had tiny heads and
tiny teeth. They all walked on four legs. But
they were different in many ways. Some
had hard plates to protect their body.
Some had a long neck. Others had a neck
that stretched high. Some had a tail club.
Others had a long tail shaped like a whip.

DINOSAUR FOSSIL FINDS

The numbers on the map on page 11 show some of the places where people have found fossils of the dinosaurs in this book. You can match each number on the map to the name and picture of the dinosaurs on this page.

1. Apatosaurus　　**2. Argentinosaurus**　　**3. Brachiosaurus**　　**4. Diplodocus**

5. Saltasaurus　　**6. Seismosaurus**　　**7. Shunosaurus**

The giant plant eaters lived in more places than any other dinosaur group. People have found **fossils** of giant plant eaters in North America, South America, Asia, Africa, Australia, and Europe.

Fossils are traces left by animals and plants
that have died. Scientists study bones,
teeth, and footprints that have turned to
stone to understand how the giant plant
eaters lived. Fossils of eggs and unborn
baby dinosaurs show how they grew.

BIG, BIGGER, BIGGEST

The two dinosaurs that chew on these tree branches stand higher than a building with five floors. They are *Brachiosaurus*, the tallest of all dinosaurs.

Scientists think that *Brachiosaurus* and other giant plant eaters swallowed stones called gastroliths. In the stomach, gastroliths rubbed against the plants a dinosaur ate. Rubbing helped break plants into tiny pieces to be used as food.

An incredibly long plant eater stretches out across the land in search of food. *Seismosaurus* is longer than 4 school buses and as heavy as 10.

Seismosaurus was the longest dinosaur. It grew 125 feet or longer from its tiny head to its whiplike tail. Its name means "the earth shaker."

The ground trembles with the approach of
the heaviest animal ever to move on land.
This plant eater is *Argentinosaurus.* It is as
heavy as a blue whale and as big as an
elementary school!

How did such huge animals find enough to eat? They may have fed on the rich seeds in the cones of evergreen trees. They may have also **migrated** to find food. Animals that migrate move to new areas as the seasons change.

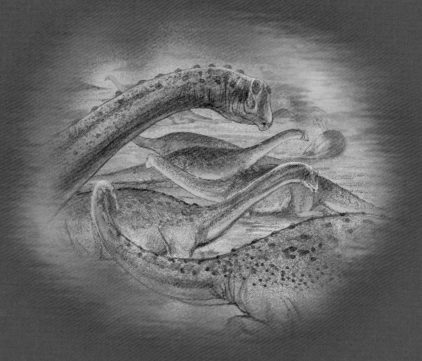

GIANT LIVES

All the dinosaurs we know of hatched from eggs. Most kinds of dinosaurs laid eggs in a nest. After hatching, the babies depended on their parents for food and care. But some giant plant eaters laid eggs in lines as they walked, not in a nest.

Apatosaurus may have laid its eggs this way. The babies that hatched from these eggs had to live on their own right away. Their parents had moved on long ago.

Some plant eaters did lay their eggs in nests. Scientists have found fossils of a nesting place for thousands of giant plant eaters in Argentina, a country in South America. The nests stretched one after another for more than a mile.

Inside many of the eggs are fossils of unborn baby dinosaurs. Most fossils show only bones. But these fossils include skin that turned to stone.

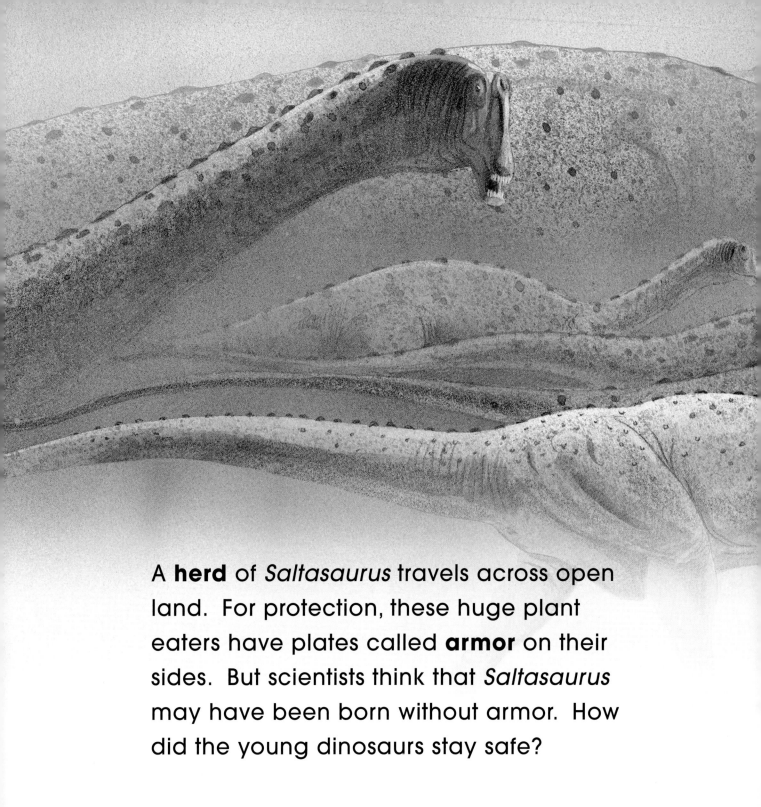

A **herd** of *Saltasaurus* travels across open land. For protection, these huge plant eaters have plates called **armor** on their sides. But scientists think that *Saltasaurus* may have been born without armor. How did the young dinosaurs stay safe?

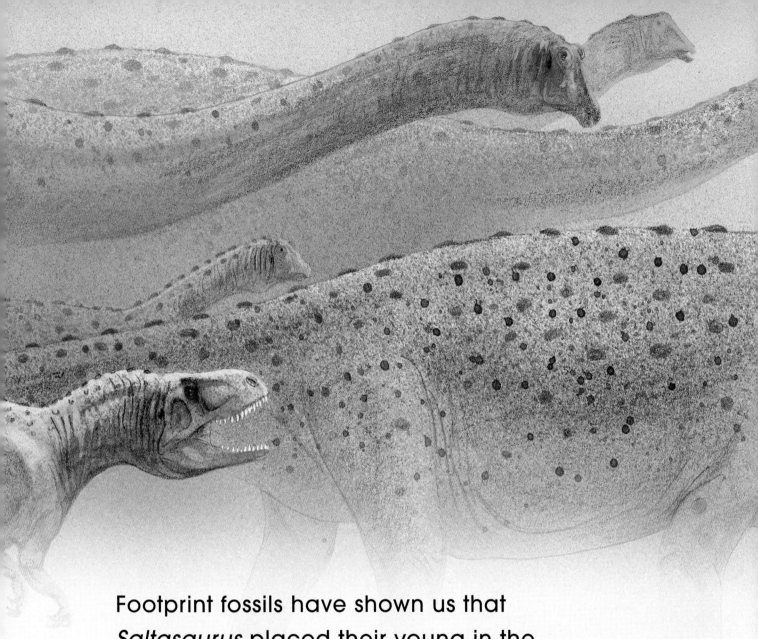

Footprint fossils have shown us that
Saltasaurus placed their young in the
center of the herd. The youngsters were
shielded from attack by the many huge
adults around them.

A *Shunosaurus* is under attack by a pack of hungry *Gasosaurus*. The plant eater swings its long tail at the hunters. A heavy ball of bone at the end of the tail whizzes through the air.

Most giant plant eaters had no tail club or other weapons. These dinosaurs stayed safe simply because they were too big for most other dinosaurs to kill.

A *Diplodocus* whips its long, thin tail as an *Allosaurus* closes in. The tail doesn't strike *Allosaurus*. But it moves through the air so quickly that it makes a booming sound.

Was this tail boom enough to frighten away an attacker like *Allosaurus?* We don't know for sure. But scientists think it may have been.

GIANT DISCOVERIES

The giant plant eaters survived to the very end of dinosaur time, 65 million years ago. No one knows for sure why the dinosaurs died out at that point. We do know that giant plant eaters left behind many clues about their lives.

We have known about some giant plant
eaters for many years. But fossils of
Argentinosaurus were not found until 1988.
The piece of an *Argentinosaurus* backbone
in the middle of this picture is larger than you
are! Can you guess where it was found?

I worked with scientists and artists in Argentina to rebuild the first skeleton of *Argentinosaurus.* First, the team dug up the bones and cleaned them. Artists made copies of the bones called casts. The real bones were kept safe for scientists to study.

Next we placed metal rods through the cast bones. The rods were put together to build the skeleton in a museum. The biggest of all dinosaurs stands again!

GLOSSARY

armor (AR-mur): bony plates on the bodies of some dinosaurs

fossils (FAH-suhlz): the remains, tracks, or traces of something that lived long ago

herbivores (URB-uh-vohrz): animals that eat plants

herd (HURD): a group of animals that live, eat, and travel together

migrated (MY-gray-tehd): moved from one place to another in order to survive

INDEX